IS THAT YOU, GOD?

A TASTE OF

DISCERNING THE VOICE OF GOD

BY

PRISCILLA SHIRER

12-20-09

To
Val Marie

From:
David

Published by LifeWay Press®
© 2009 · Priscilla Shirer

ISBN 978-1-4158-6691-7
Item 005189425

Dewey decimal classification: 231.7
Subject headings: GOD \ HOLY SPIRIT \
SPIRITUAL LIFE

Printed in the United States of America

Leadership and Adult Publishing
LifeWay Church Resources
One LifeWay Plaza
Nashville, TN 37234-0175

CONTENTS

INTRODUCTION

Over the years I've encountered many believers from different walks of life, social backgrounds, and church denominations who share one powerful desire: they want to hear God speak. Many, however, struggle to tune in to what the Lord has to say. Perhaps even more frustrating, they aren't even certain when He's speaking and when their own mental dialogues are chiming in. Before we begin our journey, let's keep in mind the wisdom of one of my favorite authors, A. W. Tozer: "Those who do not [really] believe God speaks specifically will simply ignore or explain away all the times when God does communicate with them. However, those who spend each day in a profound awareness that God does speak are in a wonder-ful position to receive His words."

Before you read any further, let me assure you of an important point. To not speak con-tradicts God's nature. The second person of the Trinity, Jesus Christ, is called the Word (see John 1:1). That designation stands at odds with silence. God loved you enough to die for you; He loves you enough to communicate with you. The Lord can and will speak to you if you've placed your faith in Jesus. First, however, you must expect and anticipate that the divine voice of God can ring in your ears and heart.

Throughout this booklet we will focus on the Holy Spirit's role in tuning our spiritual ears to the sound of God's voice. Often in our time together you'll discover references to the Lord as our Shepherd and to us as His sheep. This visual is important to our discussion because Christ used it to point out something crucial to His fellowship with us: communication thrives on relationship. "My sheep hear My voice," He said, "I know them, and they follow Me" (John 10:27).

In the Middle-Eastern sheepfolds of Jesus' day, many flocks huddled together for the evening in a common sheepfold. One shepherd, resting his body across the opening of the fold, would act as a gate and as a protector for the sheep throughout the night. In the morning individual shepherds would come to retrieve their sheep and to relieve the watchman. Each shepherd would call across the woolly backs of all the animals, summoning some to his side. Only those who belonged to him, those who had a relationship with him, would recognize their shepherd's call.

To be part of the Good Shepherd's flock, to be attuned to His voice, you must submit to God's authority over you, His child. When you accept that Christ died on the cross to bridge the gap between sinful you and the Lord, you become a part of God's family: one of His much-loved sheep. When this happens, "You are no longer [an] outsider (exile, migrant, [and] alien, excluded from the rights of citizens), but you ... share citizenship with the saints (God's own people, consecrated and set apart for Himself)." (Eph. 2:19, AMP). In short, you belong to God's household.

Many people of varying religious beliefs and backgrounds claim to access God's voice on matters ranging from what the weather will do to which nation they should conquer. Let me clarify: God in His glory can speak to any heart and declare Himself divine through the beauty of nature. But while Scripture tells us a general revelation about God is available to all humans, the daily communication line between God's mouth and the human spirit works only when an individual accepts salvation through Christ.

Nature speaks of the attributes of God, but it cannot speak individualized truths and revelations regarding life and purpose. If a person does not know Jesus, he or she is deaf to God's personalized word. Even the Pharisees, the religious "greats" of Jesus' time, were unable to understand the Truth He spoke because they refused to accept Him as God's Son (see John 8:39-47).

I don't know about you, but I want God's specific revelation to flow through my heart to impact my choices and path. When I say I want to hear from God, I mean that I need to know what job He wants me to take. I need to know what spouse He wants me to marry. I need to know whether He's calling me into full-time ministry or if He wants me to stay on my full-time, corporate job. I need to know if I'm supposed to buy this house or that one. I need to know if I'm supposed to live in Chicago or Dallas. I need specifics. I'm looking for details.

Fifteen times the New Testament records, "He who has ears to hear, let him hear" (Matt 13:9, NKJV). These passages refer not to a physical ear but to a spiritual ear that only develops when individualized relationship forms between God and man. Those of us who've accepted Christ "have an ear"; our job is to lean in and listen.

All Christ-followers are equipped with a powerful tool that attunes our spiritual ears to the Lord's voice. The Holy Spirit is like an IFB—the tiny device news anchors wear in their ears so that their producers can guide their interviews and give them tips on how to better play to the camera. When you become a Christian, you receive the supernatural ability to hear God's guidance and specific direction for your life. Whether you are in the midst of a job interview, cleaning the house, disciplining the kids, or trying to solve a conflict with your spouse, you can receive guidance on what the Lord would have you say as well as how He would have you react.

I live in awe that the God of the universe wants to talk to me, but I am so glad that He does! As we study the Holy Spirit's awesome role in connecting our ears to God's heart, lay aside the doubts. Let go of your fears. Quiet your mind.

Hush.

Our Shepherd calls ...

CHAPTER I

THE

MIRACLE

OF THE

HOLY

SPIRIT

In Matthew 17:1-5 Jesus took Peter, James, and John up a high mountain. He called those few aside to experience something incredible. This event is known as the transfiguration. The disciples recorded it as a time when Jesus' clothes shone like the sun and His face glowed like lightening. The awesomeness of God's presence radiated from Him as His divine glory was revealed before the eyes of His closest followers. Even Moses and Elijah showed up in the midst of the display. "This is My beloved Son … ," God announced over the scene, "Listen to Him" (v. 5).

This command extends past the original hearers and to modern disciples. But without the Lord's physical presence to walk beside us, how can we be expected to hear His voice?

Old and New Testament Scriptures provide an account of the miraculous ways God spoke to His children throughout early history. Moses' burning bush experience and the transfiguration stand as two of the most dramatic. I often wish that a visible sign, like the cloud that led the children of Israel by day or the pillar of fire that led them by night, would supernaturally appear in my life when I need to make a decision. So far, that hasn't happened. I have, however, heard a still small voice speaking to my heart over various situations.

Interestingly, when God chose to speak in the Bible, those who heard didn't doubt whether God had spoken or what He was asking them to do. He made His Word clear as He spoke to "our forefathers through the prophets at many times and in various ways" (Heb. 1:1, NIV). Just as He did in times long past, God wants us to hear, recognize, and obey His voice today. We too can walk in the assurance that what we hear comes from Him. But before we can do that, we need to understand the Messenger and the primary method through which He chooses to communicate today: the Holy Spirit.

Prior to His ascension, Jesus assured followers that He would send a "Comforter" to guide us in Truth. In John 16:13, the Lord explained that the Spirit would speak and encourage believers when He was no longer physically present to do so: "But when He, the Spirit of truth, comes, He will guide you into all the truth; for He will not speak on His own initiative; but whatever He hears, He will speak; and He will disclose to you what is to come." In short, the Holy Spirit relays God's messages to our hearts, whispering God's wisdom into our spiritual ears. Those promptings help guide us.

In the Old Testament, the Holy Spirit was only given to specific people to achieve specific tasks, as in the case of Moses and the Hebrew elders (see Num. 11:16-29). Old Testament believers had to count on external means to hear God because they didn't have continuous access to the Holy Spirit.

The disciples didn't see losing Jesus as an advantage, but He said they would be better off after He was gone (see John 16:7). Why? The Holy Spirit would serve as a constant source of companionship and guidance in the lives of all those who believe. He would reveal the mind of God to each person continuously and individually (see 1 Cor. 2:10). While we may often wish we enjoyed the sometimes mind-boggling access to God's plan that the Old Testament believers experienced, I believe they would choose the blessing we as modern believers share: direct, personal access to God.

You see, all of the fullness and power and the greatness and the character of God the Father rest in the Holy Spirit. That same Spirit actually takes up residence in our hearts when we become believers. He is our Comforter, our Counselor, our Helper, our Intercessor, our Advocate, and our Strength. The Holy Spirit is a personal guide who constantly draws our thoughts and hearts more in line with God's plans.

In the introduction, I mentioned that each believer is equipped with the Holy Spirit's counsel in much the same way that television station reporters have listening devices placed in their ears. Through the course of our discussion, we'll focus on this type of God-to-man interaction. But, as author Dallas Willard said, "Far be it from me to deny that spectacular experiences occur or that they are, sometimes at least, given by God."[1] I believe as he, however, that "the still small voice— or the interior or inner voice, as it is also called—is the preferred and most valuable form of individualized communication for God's purposes."

The Lord can speak to us using any method He chooses, but I rarely hear about God speaking in the miraculous ways He chose to communicate to Old Testament believers. When, for instance, was the last time you saw an altar consumed by the fire of God's approval (see 1 Chron. 21:26)? We've got to understand that our limited experiences don't mean God no longer speaks miraculously. While God chooses to speak predominately through His Spirit and His Word, we must leave room for God to be God. He alone can choose how He speaks to us. In any case, a spoken or miraculous word from God will serve as confirmation of the message of Scripture. If God uses sensational means to speak, it only confirms what His Word says.

Not long ago I sensed the Lord wanted to take me in a new direction spiritually and personally. My husband and I needed to make some decisions regarding our ministry that would stretch my faith and challenge me. It would be far more comfortable for me to stay where I was and cling to what God had already done in the past. But in my prayer time and Bible study, I sensed the Holy Spirit pulling me forward. As I attended a new Bible study during this time, the "IFB" in my spiritual ear began to hum.

I didn't know anyone in the group and no one knew me. At the end of the message, the teacher looked my direction and said, "I feel prompted to share Isaiah 43:18-19 with you. It says, 'Forget about what's happened. Don't keep going over old history. Be alert, be present. I'm about to do something brand new. It's bursting out, don't you see it?'" He continued, "The Lord wants to do something new in your life.

What He has accomplished in your life has been extraordinary, but He doesn't want you to cling to it anymore. He has something new for you, your family, and your ministry." This message confirmed what the Holy Spirit had been telling my heart.

Don't miss this critical point. When we think we hear the Spirit speaking to us about a matter, we should wisely listen for confirmation. One of the best ways to do this is to get in the Word. The Bible is God's love letter to us. What better way to know a message reflects His heart than to find it confirmed in His letter?

Constantly immersing ourselves in Scripture serves another important purpose, too. It builds the strength of our relationship with the Lord. In John 10:27 Jesus mentioned that He "know[s]" His sheep. The word "know" here is vital because relationship determines whether or not an animal will respond to its shepherd's voice. I believe our intimate knowledge of Christ goes hand-in-hand with our ability to hear and follow through on His plans for us.

In researching the unique bond between sheep and their shepherds, I called a friend who works with livestock. I asked him to explain the details of his relationship with the ewes, rams, and their young. Expecting to hear stories supporting my childhood Sunday School visions of Bible-time sheep herders slinging lost lambs over their shoulders and gazing at the stars, I was disappointed. "To be honest," he admitted with a sigh, "my sheep do not recognize my voice at all. I don't spend time with my sheep. I don't have to with the advances in modern technology. Priscilla, I could go and stand at my fence and call my sheep 'til I am blue in the face. Not one of them will pay any attention to me because they don't know my voice. They don't know my voice because we haven't spent time together."

In Exodus 34:14 of *The New Living Translation*, the Lord says, "I am God, and I'm just passionate about one thing: My relationship with you" (paraphrase). A desire for intimacy characterizes God's interactions with man from Genesis to Revelation. If you want to hear the Lord and know beyond doubt that what you hear is straight from His heart, you must make your life a continuing quest to know more of Him.

Open your Bible and cuddle up to the Shepherd. Through the power of His Holy Spirit, He'll sing words of encouragement and whisper loving guidance that will change your life.

---

[1] Dallas Willard, Hearing God: *Developing a Conversational Relationship with God* (Downers Grove, IL: Intervarsity Press, 1999), 89.

CHAPTER 2

THE RELATIONSHIP BETWEEN CONSCIENCE AND THE SPIRIT

Every human has a deep inner voice called a conscience. This voice guides and directs our choices. It's that sense deep inside that you should or shouldn't do or say something. Even non-Christians can be moral people—those who might say, "God will let me into Heaven because I'm a good person." Unfortunately, while the conscience can help direct good choices, it is flawed. We cannot equate the conscience itself with the Holy Spirit.

The problem with following only a conscience is that every person's conscience is formed and developed based on their personal environment and specific life circumstances. Each person's conscience is shaped by the tradition and truth or lies to which it has been exposed.

Consider, for example, my friend, Rebecca. She was reared in a home where all the women divorced. In her family, divorcing for trivial reasons and remarrying was the norm. As a result, she learned to think of divorce as a normal and acceptable part of the relationship between spouses. She struggles with thoughts of divorce because of the tradition of her family. Influenced by years of negative ideas toward marriage, her conscience nags at her to abandon her husband.

As in Rebecca's case, our consciences can be shaped in a way that is not pleasing to the Lord. Maybe our parents were verbally abusive so we mentally approve negative words to our own kids. Maybe we grew up believing that wealthy people were selfish and that stealing from them is OK should we find ourselves in less fortunate circumstances. We may believe it's acceptable to defraud them in business, too. We've got to realize that sinful influences warp our God-given consciences, hindering our ability to rely on conscience alone. We desperately need the Holy Spirit's guidance in bringing our thoughts and consciences in line with God's Word.

When you become a Christian, your spirit becomes new (2 Cor. 5:17). You don't become changed, you become exchanged. The Spirit of the living God dwells in your human spirit.

He gives you new life (see Titus 3:5). That life extends to your conscience as the Holy Spirit begins to speak over the damage sin did to your sense of right and wrong. Where it was once OK to overeat, for instance, you may suddenly feel convicted about gluttony. Where it was once acceptable to watch shows promoting immoral behavior, you may find yourself feeling ashamed by the glorification of adultery. In each similar instance, you experience the Holy Spirit making sure that you begin thinking and acting more like Christ, that the things that make His heart hurt cause pain to yours, and that the things that bring Him joy bring joy to you.

In Romans 9:1 the Apostle Paul said, "My conscience testifies with me in the Holy Spirit." Paul realized that the Spirit had laid a hand on his broken conscience, shaken it awake, and insisted that it join Him in the work of making Paul more like Jesus. While this was a progressive event that reshaped his conscience over time and not immediately, Paul felt the change acutely enough to recognize that his life and actions following his salvation were in line with God's plans.

One of the most common questions I encounter on the topic of discerning God's voice is, "How do I know what I'm hearing is from God and not my own conscience?" Below are a list of guidelines we can follow to help us be sure we truly hear the Spirit instead of warped conscience. I call them the five Ms of correctly hearing God.

1. Look for the message of the Spirit. Listen to the Holy Spirit. Don't just casually ask God for guidance. Consciously turn your attention inward to see if what you are sensing carries the weight of God or if it is the unsure, unsteady voice of your own plans.

2. Live in the mode of prayer. Submit what you hear back to God in prayer. Through-out your day when the issue comes to

your mind, don't spend time worrying; spend time handing the matter over to the Lord.

3. Search out the model of Scripture. Carefully consider the Scriptures. Does what you think you're hearing in any way contradict the character of God or His Word?

4. Submit to the ministry of a mentor. Seek the counsel of a wise, more mature believer who can discern God's leading in his or her own life.

5. Expect the mercy of confirmation. Ask the Lord for confirmation. God desires for you to know His will. He's not hiding it from you. When I ask the Lord to confirm what He is saying to me through the Holy Spirit so I can be sure He is indeed speaking, He allows the Spirit to speak to me and verify His message through His written Word, circumstances, or even another person.

Author Philip Yancey made a great observation on this topic. He said, "I know the Lord is speaking to me when I stop listening to sounds from the world that feed my sense of pride and ambition. Instead, I fall quiet ... and sometimes the Spirit speaks, awakening my conscience, reminding me of failures, stirring my compassion and sense of justice, aligning me with God's will." Yancey realized that God's voice always aligns us with what He wants. Anytime that little voice we hear approves a selfish plan over one that glorifies God, we are not hearing from the Lord.

A few days ago I felt God showing me that He wanted to cut some things from my life so I could focus more on my relationship with Him. After seeking Him in prayer, I asked Him for confirmation. My Bible study that day was on Deuteronomy 30:6: "The LORD your God will circumcise your heart and the heart of your descendants, to love the LORD your God with all your heart and with all your soul, in order that you may live." When I opened a book later that day, the section I was reading was entitled "A Circumcised Heart." At Bible study that week, my leader told me he sensed I was about to experience a shaking in my life for the purpose of getting rid of that which kept me from being fully God's. The Lord emphatically confirmed His word.

Over the past year and a half, I've grown so encouraged by the many incredible books I've found on discerning God's voice. Over and over they parrot the wisdom of saints who listen to God's voice daily. Their shared thoughts on how to discern God's voice come down to this: You'll never get it 100 percent right. The only way to ever be 100 percent sure that God has spoken is after the fact, when looking back to see the hand of God and how He leads us down life's path.

As long as we live in this fallen world, we'll never be perfect at discerning God's voice. Don't let that discourage you. Let it free you to trust that God is big enough and in control enough to take care of you and to cover you in His mercy and grace. Our job as sheep of God's fold is not to have all the answers but to press against the Shepherd from whom we'll learn as we go. The better we know Him, the better we'll follow His plans and trust His heart over our own.

IS THAT YOU, GOD?

CHAPTER 3

THE

HOLY SPIRIT:

TRUSTWORTHY

GUIDE

I take many plane rides, but one stands out in my memory. I was enjoying the ride and reading a book as the plane sailed through the air. Suddenly we were shaken from our seats as the aircraft seemed to fall for a few moments before regaining composure. Passengers screamed, overhead compartments opened, and bags flew across the aisles.

After a few moments the pilot explained. The control tower had radioed to tell him we were on a collision course with another airplane. If we didn't take immediate evasive action, people would hear about a major disaster on the evening news. The pilot apologized but told us it was his only option to keep us safe. The control tower's ability to see the whole picture and the pilot's willingness to trust its guidance saved our lives.

The Holy Spirit is like a control tower that keeps our ears connected with God's all-seeing and all-knowing wisdom. The Lord sees the end as well as the beginning and seeks to guide us with His insight.

Unfortunately, most of us balk at the Spirit's guidance at some time or another. Unlike the pilot who so wisely followed the directions ground control sent, we begin to think the Lord may not have quite as firm a handle on the situation as we do. We question whether He truly understands a matter from all angles. We live in fear that He just might let us down. As a result, we sometimes shrug off His guidance.

A friend recently admitted her struggles with this issue. "Priscilla," she said. "I want to hear God's voice, but to be honest, I'm just afraid He's not as good as we'd like to believe. I'm not sure I can trust Him." My friend spoke out of hurt. Twice abandoned at the altar, her broken heart led her to conclude that God was not really good. She forgot His promise in Jeremiah 29:11: "'For I know the plans I have for you,' declares the LORD, "plans to prosper you and not to harm you, plans to give you hope and a future'" (NIV).

In his book *A Shepherd's Look at Psalm 23*, Phillip Keller explained that a competent shepherd took care of his sheep. He tended their fleeces, rotated their pastureland, monitored their health, and sought pure water for them. In every instance he cared for their needs and looked out for their best interests. How much better, then, will our Good Shepherd—and the Lord is most definitely that—take care of us when we choose to follow His loving guidance?

Understand that the Shepherd longs for us to experience His love and protection. He always has our best interests and His glory in mind. Never do believers need to fear that the Spirit is on a break or unwilling to guide us down the right path. But we've got to yield to His control.

Most of us don't blatantly set out to ignore the Spirit's leading. Instead, we try to become our own control towers. We think we don't need a shepherd. We want to do what feels good, appeases our emotions, seems rational to our minds, and suits our wills—with little thought to what the Lord advises. We've got to realize that The Holy Spirit sees the whole picture and may want to reveal something beyond what our physical senses can comprehend.

To insist on doing things our way over God's way is foolish. Consider this illustration. The plotline of the 1960s television show *The Beverly Hillbillies* revolved around the story of Jed Clampett, a rough-around-the-edges man who lived on a piece of land that turned out to be extremely valuable. Until a stray bullet from his hunting rifle revealed the presence of oil on his land, Jed lived like a hillbilly. Immediately upon its discovery, however, Jed moved his family to a place of wealth and easy living. Now suppose Jed chose to ignore the cash that oil brought in. How frustrating we would find his story had Clampett insisted on living on his pre-oil strike income for all his days! What if he'd chosen to keep living by the pittance his own efforts brought in when access to plenty lay within his reach?

Sadly, many of us walk around like spiritual hillbillies when we've got the power and the fullness and the greatness of God available to us.

The Spirit's guidance is part of our inheritance as Christ-followers. In Ephesians 1:13 Paul tells believers that we are sealed with the Holy Spirit, as if the Spirit's presence in our lives provides official proof and security in our relationships with God. Paul continues (and I'm paraphrasing here), "I'm praying for you constantly. I am asking God, the glorious Father of our Lord Jesus Christ, to allow you to realize the oil mine you are living on." So that, he continues, "you will be given all spiritual wisdom and understanding so that you might grow in your knowledge of God. I pray that your hearts will be flooded with light so that you can understand the wonderful future He has promised to those He called. I want you to realize what a rich and glorious inheritance He has given to His people. I pray that you will begin to understand the incredible greatness of His power for us who believe Him. This is the same mighty power that raised Christ from the dead and seated Him in the place of honor at God's right hand in the heavenly realms."

Essentially, Paul says, "Hey! You fellow Christians sit on a spiritual gold mine! You can tap into the same power that raised Jesus from the tomb! I want you to see the Spirit's influence as a part of your inheritance. I want you to tap into His power so you can grow in your relationship with God." Paul appreciated the Spirit's importance. He desperately wanted others to do the same.

In 1 Corinthians 2:6-7 we get further insight into Paul's understanding of how the Spirit can guide us. "I do speak with words of wisdom" he says, "but not the kind of wisdom that belongs to this world ... No, the wisdom we speak of is the mystery of God—his plan that was previously hidden" In verses 10-13 he continues, "It was to us that God revealed these things by his Spirit. For his Spirit searches out everything and shows us God's deep secrets. No one can know ... God's thoughts except God's own Spirit. And we have received God's Spirit (not the world's spirit), so we can know the wonderful things God has freely given us" (NLT).

Paul gives us a glimpse of all the wonderful riches available to us as God's children. He says there's a hidden wisdom that the smartest person you know can't access. It's a wealth of divinely inspired understanding that will help you answer life's toughest questions and face its difficulties with confidence. This wealth comes not because you graduated from a certain school but because you've connected with the Holy Spirit. I agree with Paul: We can't afford to tune the Spirit out! He is our guide—the only guide worth having. We've got to trust the Control Tower.

So how can we learn to focus on the messages the Spirit sends? We begin by daily surrendering ourselves to Him and asking Him to heighten our spiritual senses. Then, as we do the mundane tasks that consume our lives, we purposefully turn our awareness inward and say, "God, what do you think about that? What should I do about this? What should I say in this situation?" As surely as winter follows autumn, the Lord will guide the decisions and responses of those determined to trust in Him.

As God's children and the sheep of His fold, we've got to retrain ourselves to let the Spirit guide and dominate our decision making. The Holy Spirit has begun the work of sanctifying you so that your desires more closely mirror His. When you obediently spend time getting to know Him, you say, "Yes, I am committed to cooperating with You, Lord."

I've found that as I put my attention on the Spirit, something miraculous takes place. Not only do I become more able to clearly distinguish God's word to me, but I find a wonderful sense of peace. Like the pilot on my heart-jarring flight, we can position ourselves for success and safety. We can live in the peaceful reassurance that God is in control.

IS THAT YOU, GOD?

CHAPTER 4

THE

ONGOING

TRANSFORMATION

PROCESS

We know the Holy Spirit works a miracle as He renews our consciences and awakens us to His guidance. The Bible is clear that we are actually renewed as the Lord takes up residence in our lives. The problem some find, however, is that total transformation never seems to happen. In spite of our most dedicated efforts to walk as the Lord would have us walk, in spite of our deepest determination not to sin, in spite of the fact that we are God's children and truly love Him, we sometimes fall flat on our spiritual faces. How then, you may ask, can we know that we are truly transformed?

First, know that we don't receive the Spirit in installment plans. We receive all we're going to have of Him the moment we accept Christ. Understand, too, that the Christian life is one of ongoing transformation. We are equipped with everything we need to grow in godliness. But while we may have all of the Spirit, He may not have all of us. Here lies the root of the problem.

You include three parts. Your spirit allows contact with the spiritual realm. Your soul allows you access to your emotions and mind. Your body relates with the physical realm through the five senses. As you yield to and obey the Holy Spirit's leading in your life, He conforms your soul to the image of Christ and uses your body as the instrument to carry out His purposes. Sometimes, however, we choose to deafen ourselves to His leading. When we do, we start to look less transformed and more in need of reform.

Some time ago as we left the airport, my husband's finger got caught in a rotating door. When we finally got it out, Jerry claimed he couldn't feel the tip of his finger. A visit to the doctor revealed that he had severed a nerve.

Every time we decide not to obey God, we start damaging the connection between our ears and His heart. Make no mistake; God doesn't go anywhere. Just as Jerry's brain continued to send messages to his damaged finger, the Spirit continues to attempt communication with our hardening hearts. After a while, however, we may start to wonder why we aren't hearing His voice. We'll even find it gets easier and easier to commit sins as we turn blind eyes on the Spirit's red flags of conviction. Our sin problem acts like radio static that hinders our ability to clearly hear the Spirit's leading.

I can't begin to tell you how many times I have thought the spiritual nerve between my ears and God's mouth was damaged to the point that I could no longer discern the Lord's voice. But what I didn't tell you about my husband's injury is that after some time, the feeling did return in his damaged finger. God can restore spiritual nerve damage, too. No matter how distant you may feel from Him in a given moment, you can know that He's waiting to repair you and restore you so you can better hear His word for your life.

If you find yourself in a position where you think you can't hear God, talk to Him about it. Admit the places where you know you've been living your way instead of His. Tell Him that you desire sensitivity to the Holy Spirit's leading in your life. Never allow feelings of discouragement to hinder you from pressing closer to God in prayer. He loves you. He wants to heal you. He wants to draw you close.

Everyone faces times of spiritual highs and lows. Even when we determine to follow Christ and listen and try to obey as the Holy Spirit tells us what is best for us, our flesh sometimes pulls us down the opposite path. Paul, one of the godliest men in history, shared this struggle. He writes in Romans 7:14-19 (NIV) one of the clearest descriptions of the battle between the flesh's tendency toward sin and obedience to the Spirit:

> *We know that the law is spiritual; but I am unspiritual, sold as a slave to sin. I do not understand what I do. For what I want to do I do not do, but what I hate I do. And if I do what I do not want to do, I agree that the law is good. As it is, it is no longer I myself who do*

it, but it is sin living in me. I know that noth-
ing good lives in me, that is, in my sinful nature.
For I have the desire to do what is good, but I
cannot carry it out. For what I do is not the
good I want to do; no, the evil I do not want to
do—this I keep on doing.

The Book of James was written to believers whose spirits had already been made new through salvation. But the author gave the believers startling instructions in James 1:21: "Get rid of all moral filth and the evil that is so prevalent and humbly accept the word planted in you, which can save you" (NIV). James tells us our souls still need to be saved. The soul still contains "filthiness and all that remains of wickedness" (NASB). This gets to the heart of Paul's struggle—a struggle that all believers face.

Have you ever sat in front of a piece of chocolate cake or some other indulgence and felt you couldn't help but take a bite? You know, one of those moments when you want to stick to your diet but the aroma of dessert overrides better sense? I know sometimes my stomach can be completely full but my mouth is determined to taste the chocolate. Even though I know I'll soon regret my decision, I find myself picking up the fork for bite after delicious bite. This is not unlike the struggle we face when we choose sinful tendencies over God's ways.

In Romans 12:1, Paul tells us how to experience victory with our bodies as we seek to follow the leading of the Spirit. He says, "Present your bodies a living and holy sacrifice." Paul didn't say to experience victory in this area you have to fight really hard. He just said to present, to yield, or to surrender your body. Through Jesus you have already been given victory as a gift (see 1 Cor. 15:57). You experience it by presenting your body to God as an instrument for His use.

The Holy Spirit is always busy making us like Jesus, but we must cooperate in the effort. We must remind ourselves that every part of our bodies was given to us not for our own gratification but as an "instrument to do what is right for the glory of God" (Rom. 6:13, NLT). An African missionary once explained that each morning, before he got up, he took time to present himself to the Lord. He stretched out across his bed and pictured it as an altar on which he was the sacrifice. He started each day by saying, "Lord, this day I present myself as a tool for You. Today I am Your living sacrifice."

Why is this important to a discussion on being transformed by the Spirit? Kay Arthur explains, "I believe in the truth found in Romans 12:1-2. If I have presented my body to Him as a living sacrifice, and I have, and I'm being transformed by the renewing of my mind then I'm able to prove—to put to the text—what His will is. He will show me that which is good, acceptable, and perfect for me." You see, if we want to be transformed, we've got to get on board. We need to let our lives demonstrate to the Lord our willingness to follow Him in spite of sin's frustrating and ever present pull.

My husband was satisfied with his corporate job when out of nowhere God told him to leave so we could work together in ministry. Jerry thought it absurd. He had worked a normal 8–5 job with good pay and benefits most of his life and was quickly climbing the ladder of success at his company. Doing something unconventional like self-employed ministry seemed illogical. Yet the Holy Spirit would not let him rest. It became clear through the Spirit's leading, prayer, wise counsel, and confirmation through the Word and other circumstances that God was leading him in that direction despite the way he felt.

Often the Spirit's leading contradicts our logic and feelings; but when we submit, we will experience a deep-rooted peace about our decisions. As the Spirit conforms us to the image of Christ, the gap between His desires and ours narrows. God put His thought in Jerry's mind and, over time, Jerry's feelings radically changed. He began to feel it was foolish to stay at his old job when God was giving him an opportunity to work full time for the kingdom of God.

The Lord works in us to radically change us (see 2 Thess. 2:13). When you take in God's Word, massive renovation shakes your insides.

If you want to be transformed by the Spirit, you need to conform to doing life His way. Remember, God our Shepherd always has His glory and our good in mind.

CHAPTER 5

LETTING

HIM

LEAD

A few years ago I planned to attain my doctorate at Dallas Theological Seminary. I filled out mounds of paperwork and wrote essay after essay. Once I gathered a few last minute references, I got in the car and pulled out of the drive. Why not drop off my application packet in person?

The application lay in a brown manila envelope on the passenger's seat beside me. I was so proud of it. It represented such work. So much planning! I thought it held the key to my future. But suddenly, I heard a quiet voice whisper to my heart, "Did you decide to go to school without consulting Me, Priscilla? More education is a good thing, Priscilla, but I don't want you back in school right now."

Such authority rang in those soft-spoken words that I didn't need to question whether I was hearing from God. Though I very much wanted to pursue my dream, I immediately took the next exit and drove back home. Surprisingly, the desire to go back to school completely left me by the time I got there. Not once have I regretted the choice. Many times I've paused to thank God for it as new twists and happy surprises would've made completing a doctorate program very difficult if not impossible.

I share this story because I want to assure you that the Spirit's leading isn't some intangible thing. God does not author confusion. As you discern where to land on the many major decisions that you make, know that God will send you a red flag of conviction when He wants you to "Stop" and will send a green light of ease and peace in your life to say, "Go." We don't have to wonder what God wants for us. Remember, He wants to speak to us. That's why we've got to stay attuned. When your conscience is not clear, when you are in doubt internally, then just wait. And if you can verify what you think you hear against the Truth of God's Word, you can know that it is from the Lord.

Should I attend that kind of party? Should I go to that kind of movie? Should I participate in this kind of activity? Should I or should I not drink wine? Should I go to this particular event? Should I or should I not wear pants or makeup? What is it that the Holy Spirit would have me do? Should I get this job or that job? Every question has an answer; sometimes we need to just patiently wait for God to lead us to it. As you listen to the Holy Spirit guiding and steering your conscience, look to the Word of God and to the confirmation of His sovereign hand in your circumstances.

Before we leave this topic, I want to acknowledge that a lot of us look around every corner to discover God's will. Some go so far as to worry that they might choose the wrong sock color or order the wrong entree without His guidance. Understand that the Lord doesn't want us wringing our hands in anxiety about anything—especially not trivial matters.

Please understand that desiring and doing God's will is not our responsibility to discover; it's His responsibility to reveal. Philippians 2:13 reminds us, "For it is God who works in you to will and to act according to his good purpose" (NIV). And in the Book of Philippians, Paul encouraged Philippian believers to have the attitude of perseverance—not fear— in knowing and doing God's will. Further, Paul assured them that if at any time they stepped away from what God desired, the Lord would let them know.

Through the Holy Spirit, "[God] writes His laws on our hearts and on our minds, and we love them, and are drawn, by our affections and judgment, not driven, to our obedience."[1] Submitting to the guidance of the Holy Spirit is never something to dread or to fear we might mess up. As you fall more in love with Christ and your relationship with Him deepens, you'll find that it happens naturally.

I don't need to frantically search for God's will; instead, I frantically search for God. I trust that He will show me what He wants me to do and how to do it by speaking through the Holy Spirit and the written Word. As I seek Him, stay in Scripture, and continue to keep an intimate relationship with Him by confessing my sin, He transforms my mind and emotions to align with His plans.

I will never forget reading Psalm 46:10 in February 1997. I had read this verse many times before, but this time it was as if for the first time. I was so tired that morning. As the familiar words of this verse washed over me, I saw it with new eyes and heard the Holy Spirit speak, "Cease striving and know that I am God." A feeling of peace and serenity washed over me as the Lord removed my burden. I knew the Holy Spirit had caused me to truly understand the verse. It became relevant for me. The Lord wrote His law on my mind. That day I also discovered the beautiful truth of 2 Corinthians 3:17 "Where the Spirit of the Lord is, there is freedom" (NIV).

Once I struggled with the need to have the last word in what I call "heated discussions" with my husband, Jerry. Often we'd discuss one issue or another and it would turn into an argument as we went back and forth with each other. I'd get to a point in the debate where I'd listen to him talk and mentally rail, *You don't know what you're talking about!* No sooner did he pause for breath than I'd shut the argument down with my answer, my last word. Sometimes I couldn't wait for him to be finished with his point so I could lay it on him.

Prior to one of these discussions, the Holy Spirit had begun prepping my heart. He started reshaping me on this point as I read "Be completely humble and gentle; ... bearing with one another in love" (Eph. 4:2, NIV); and "give preference to one another in honor" (see Rom. 12:10); and "Wives, submit to your husbands as to the Lord (Eph. 5:22, NIV)." Within a week, I found myself heating up for another discussion with Jerry over some little thing or another and I felt something inside of me say, "No. No, Priscilla. You may win this little battle, but you won't build a healthy marriage this way. Remember this passage? Remember what God said in Ephesians? Would you rather win this argument or allow him to be the man of your house?"

As if someone knocked a physical weight off my shoulders, I felt myself sag with relief. I didn't have to argue with my husband. I didn't have to have the last word. I did need to obey God's Word. When I decided to shut my mouth and cuddle up to my husband's side instead, I felt the Spirit's presence as refreshing as a cool breeze on a hot day.

I'm not saying that I should never share an opinion that differs from my husband's. My point is that each day, as I humbly submit my way to God's in all things, I see that the Holy Spirit is slowly but surely changing my tastes to suit what pleases Him. When I delight myself in God, I can relax in knowing that He will speak clearly, order my steps, and cause me to desire what brings Him pleasure. These same freedoms are available to you as a child of God.

---

[1] Hannah Whitall Smith, *The Christian's Secret of a Happy Life* (New York City: Grosset and Dunlap, n.d.), 76.

CONCLUSION

I was taught that a relationship with God was a personal one in which He speaks to His children. I sat in many prayer meetings where passionate believers shared stirring encounters with God's voice while my own soul was filled with overwhelming confusion. How did these saints know God was speaking?

Years ago I made a decision to believe God speaks but would not disappoint myself by believing He would speak to me. I hid my growing dissatisfaction with my Bible study and powerless prayer time. I thought this was the way it would always be, until the day God spoke personally and intimately to me. An encounter with

His presence made me different: I was filled with a hunger for the presence of God.

Since that day I've determined to tune in to the sound of my Shepherd's call. I've stopped believing the Enemy's lie that I'm unable to do so. I've stopped fearing that I'll substitute my desires over God's. In Deuteronomy 30:11-14, God said, "What I am commanding you today is not too difficult for you or beyond your reach. It is not up in heaven, so that you have to ask, 'Who will ascend into heaven to get it and proclaim it to us so we may obey it?' Nor is it beyond the sea, so that you have to ask, 'Who will cross the sea to get it and proclaim it to us so we may obey it?' No, the word is very near you; it is in your mouth and in your heart so you may obey it." (NIV).

If you know beyond a shadow of a doubt you've received Jesus Christ as Savior, God wants to talk to you. But your job, your number one task in this moment, is to choose to believe that He will.

Well-tended sheep need not fear that a wolf will run off with their lambs or that the food supply will run out. They don't need to panic over where to find water or shade. They simply trust that their shepherd will meet their needs, that he will call out and give direction and guidance as needed.

Isaiah 40:11 says, "[The Lord] tends his flock like a shepherd: He gathers the lambs in his arms and carries them close to his heart" (NIV). Our spiritual ears align with the Father's heart as we grow in intimate relationship with Him.

Through the power of the Holy Spirit, tune in to the steady beat of the Father's love for you. He will not disappoint.

How do you know when

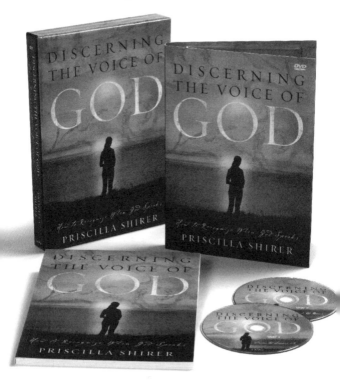

God is speaking to you?

Discerning the Voice of God—
A New Teaching Series from LifeWay

God's voice doesn't have to be a mystery. In this six-session interactive study, Priscilla Shirer teaches powerful Bible truths and offers practical steps to enable you to know the voice of God— His character, His language, His tone of voice.

As you spend time in God's Word and better understand the role of the Holy Spirit, you will learn to distinguish God's voice from all those voices chattering in the world around you—and in your head!

Personal workbook study and Priscilla's messages on DVD will help you practice key insights that will draw you closer to God.

For details, visit <u>www.lifeway.com/priscillashirer</u> or see the women's leader or Bible study leader at your church.

abundantly you | www.lifeway.com/**women**

ABOUT THE AUTHOR

PRISCILLA SHIRER focuses her Bible teaching and speaking ministry on the expository teaching of the Word of God to women. She desires for women to know the uncompromising truths of Scripture intellectually and experience them practically by the power of the Holy Spirit.

A graduate of the Dallas Theological Seminary with a Master's degree in Biblical Studies, Priscilla is now in full-time ministry to women. She is the author of *He Speaks to Me: Preparing to Hear from God* and *Discerning the Voice of God: How to Recognize When God Speaks.*

Priscilla is the daughter of pastor, speaker, and well-known author Dr. Tony Evans. She is married to her best friend, Jerry. The couple resides in Dallas with their three young sons, Jackson, Jerry Jr., and Jude.

Jerry and Priscilla have founded Going Beyond Ministries which is committed to seeing believers receive the most out of their relationships with the Lord.